MESSAGES OF TRUTH

BY

REV. NATALIE R. JEAN

DEDICATION

My journey into the spiritual world has been a very rewarding one. On this journey, I learned about the teachings of many great masters under the leadership of Rev. Dr. Christopher Bazemore and Rev. Maryse Colimon Hubert. I was yearning to be fed. I wanted to gain some soul satisfaction. My nourishment heightened further when I started studying Spiritual Science, through the teachings of Emma Curtis Hopkins. As a result my life changed tremendously and I will forever be grateful. I was inspired to write the following poems because of the wonderful gift that Emma Curtis Hopkins bestowed upon me. Her teachings have taught me to speak the Truth about myself and the world around me. Her teachings have enabled me to see Spirit everywhere.

I AM FREE!!

TABLE OF CONTENTS

In the beginning, there was simplicity to life. We walked among nature and new nothing but love. Let us go back to knowing nothing but peace and love.

NRJ

Thou art, and there is none beside Thee,
in Thine Own Omnipresence,
Omnipotence, Omniscience

Emma Curtis Hopkins
(*Voluntary Surrender*)

IN THE BEGINNING

The Perfect sound echoed the earth
Songs from God's creations
The land was green and untouched
Trees were aplenty
Oceans were sky blue
Life fed off of the land
Tranquility and Peace was all that was known
Let us turn back the hands of time
To the Beginning

We often want to blame God for all the wrong choices we make. But the Truth is that we are responsible for all our own choices. We have free will. All experiences are good, because they bring us closer to God.

NRJ

I am Thine only and I in Thee I live, move, and have my being

Emma Curtis Hopkins
(*Voluntary Surrender*)

I CHOOSE

In a world tormented by the hand of hate
I choose to see love
An appearance of a disease
Has no bearing on my soul
Because I know God has made me whole
At a time of desecration
I choose to see peace within all nations
My mind to my mind
It is only time
That consciousness of mankind
Arises to the perfect plan
The kingdom at hand
Is ours by his command
Take a stand and Choose
See the Good within all
Can't you see
He made you and me

Speaking the Truth of who you truly are is your greatest power. Lift the veil of human conditioning and set yourself free.

NRJ

Vision often Godward and live anew

Emma Curtis Hopkins
(The High Watch)

THE TRUTH SHALL SET YOU FREE

My eyes closed
Sitting here on the mountain top
I surrender to the voice within me
My heart bursts into a golden flame
Love surrounds me
The Truth has been revealed
I am Spirit
I am Love
I am born Free

Belief in fear, doubt, and anxiety leads you to believe in a separate God. There can only be One. God is the only Power.

NRJ

Gaze often toward Our Father, and all thoughts shall be like moving music

Emma Curtis Hopkins
(*The High Watch*)

WHOM DO YOU SERVE?

Guided by Spirit
Voices all around
Try and shake your ground
Follow me is what they say
Choose to look the other way
Guided by material virtues
It will promise anything just to use you
There is only one Power
That can take you higher
Believe in me is what is spoken
It can never be broken
The destined plan is set in motion
You'll never be deceived
Because Liberation is what you'll receive

You are beautiful, wise, Intelligent, abundant in all.
You embody what God is.

NRJ

Our initial and compelling faculty is our inner vision

Emma Curtis Hopkins
(The High Watch)

YOU

Teacher
Poet
Singer
Musician
Painter
Artist
Developer
Dancer
Minister
Father
Mother
Brother
Sister
Who are you?
I AM Spirit
I bring joy to the world

What you think of yourself is what people see. Choose to know that you are everything. Peace, love, and harmony.

NRJ

My God is my life

Emma Curtis Hopkins
(*Scientific Christian Mental Practice*)

THOUGHTS

From my mind to my mind
I can lead the blind
A positive thought
Leads to a positive step
No room for negations
Nor for hallucinations
Focused on Good
I can only see Good
I am on a quest
To invoking the best
What I see in you
I see in me
The God within
Beckoning you to come in

When we are born, we know where we come from. As the years go by, and the human takes over, our memories of home get buried within. But somehow, during those years, we start to yearn and crave for something deeper. Satisfaction. A way back home to the Father.

NRJ

The Kingdom of heaven is within you

Jesus Christ

HOME

We all seek to know the Truth of who we are
Whether we have traveled near or far
Home is where you long to be
A safe place for you and me
The Father always guides us through
By giving us a clue
Your home is neither near nor far
It is a place hidden deep within
It is where the greatest love resides
So close your eyes
And take a wonderful ride
The time has finally come
You've found your way home

What is rightfully yours has always been there. Open your eyes, heart, and loving arms to receive your gifts.

NRJ

I Am the Power of skill

Emma Curtis Hopkins
(Radiant I Am)

BIRTHRIGHT

Jerusalem gave birth to a Holy man
He had only one plan
To teach every woman and man
Their birthright was at hand
He said, 'walk with me to the holy land
I'll teach you about
The one in command
I am not the only begotten son
Unearthed by the sun
I AM your teacher, brother, friend
Here to make a stand
We come from the same name
I AM THAT I AM

When you decide to take the Right step, Divine Right Action has already taken place.

NRJ

I Am a tower whose Radiance is unending
Wisdom through all things

Emma Curtis Hopkins
(Radiant I Am)

EMOTION

Each step you take
He is right by your side
Even if you try to hide
When you're feeling blue
He'll show you what to do
You can scream and shout
And move all about
Loving you is all He knows
He sees you as beautiful as a rose
A ray of emotions can never turn him away
Forever He is to stay

There is nothing too hard for me. All appearances are pushed out of the Universe.

NRJ

I make my Self known by speaking,
thinking, writing, living the word of
myself

Emma Curtis Hopkins
(Radiant I Am)

<u>MOUNTAINS</u>

Desperation tries to take control
Anxiety and Fear want to take hold
On A Path of Self-Destruction
Something inside says it is time to take action
You can move Mountains
Stand Tall
You will never fall
Remember who you are
You were made in His image
Affirm your Truth
Nothing can withstand
He will never let you fall
The Power within
You can move mountains

You are never alone. Don't look up or down. I Am right within you, expressing my unwavering love.

NRJ

It shall come to pass that before they call, I will answer, and while they are yet speaking, I will hear "for this substance is named the visibility of God while we are speaking"

Emma Curtis Hopkins
(The Resurrection)

LET GO

You think of the past
And wonder why it didn't last
Words unspoken
Left you broken
It was time to part
And find a new start
The first step wouldn't be easy
Making you feel a little queasy
Letting Go
Would let you know
Any experience is a lesson learned
Bringing you closer
To the One within
You can only win
Let Go

What is this thing that wants to trap me, keeping me from my destiny. I cannot be trapped because you do not exist! God is the only Power.

NRJ

Drop fearing lest you do wrong. Be free
as you were born

Emma Curtis Hopkins
(The Gospel Series in Spiritual Science)

COME WALK WITH ME

Take my hand
Let us walk across the land
Within the desert sand
Revealing an awakening
Guided by the light
Blazing so Bright
The Divine I
Looking towards the sky
A sweet kiss from the sun
Reveals that we are one

Give in to Spirit. Let go of Ego. Receive Eternal Freedom.

NRJ

You judge not by appearances, but by righteousness

Emma Curtis Hopkins
(Scientific Christian Mental Practice)

FEAR NOT

What is this thing that tries to take hold
It can make you feel so cold
It is a terror
Created by error
Appearances that challenge the mind
Are not kind
I open my book to Psalm 91
I remember the One
Trust in Me
Is what I choose to see
Truth spoken aloud
Will lift the cloud
Under his wings I shall stay
To see another day

What you see before you is not real. Don't speak of it.
Focus on Spirit, for it is the only thing that is real.

NRJ

Faith in Goodness will feed itself and increase itself in the same way we rise and work miracles of it

Emma Curtis Hopkins
(Scientific Christian Mental Practice)

APPEARANCES

Battered and Bruised
Used and abused
I looked in the mirror
And didn't like what I saw
I was numb and raw
With patience
I sat in the silence
Hoping for an answer
It came to me then
What I chose to see wasn't real
I needed to heal
Change my conscious mind
And see the beauty hidden deep inside
In the end
I say good-bye to an old friend
And said hello to the new me

Know with no uncertainty that all you desire is yours. Knowing and believing in yourself is all you need. It is something you feel.

NRJ

The Spirit of God is the Word of Truth.
We are building the temple of our own
character

Emma Curtis Hopkins
(Scientific Christian Mental Practice)

FAITH

Illusions that try to cloud our vision
I say unwind and clear your mind
Let the clickity clack of idle chatter
Disappear like there is no matter
I AM giving in to a Higher Power
You can't touch it
Yet it is something that you feel
It is unseen
You know it is real
Spirit is All
Mother, Father
He will never let you fall
Give in to what you can't see
All will be revealed to thee

We all shine with brilliance, as beautiful as the rarest gem. Beauty is in the eye of the beholder. Spirit can only see yours. Choose to see only beauty in your neighbor.

NRJ

It is preaching remission when we tell
the unweighted light force to face that
we know our surety of unburdened life
under the healing smile

Emma Curtis Hopkins
(High Mysticism)

JEWEL

Born from the earth
Flawless, brilliant, beauty
Conceived by the heavens
The seed within a womb
Flourishes through a mother's love
Set free unto the world
Priceless
Created from the One
Love, Peace and Harmony
Nourish it
I AM a Jewel
My illumination
Spreads across the nation
A light so bright
It shines throughout the night
It cannot be dimmed
I AM protected by Him
I AM a Jewel
Brought by the Light

A flame within ready to burst. Feel it's warm embrace. God loving you.

NRJ

Substance is God

Emma Curtis Hopkins
(Scientific Christian Mental Practice)

LIGHT

White light so bright
Hold me tight
Into the night
I am not going to fight
My path is clear
There is nothing to fear
Resurrected
And ready to be led
Souls are waiting
To be risen from the dead
The Truth is what I preach
That you are never out of reach

Healing waters nourish our land and our souls. Let it touch your skin and feel the heavenly presence.

NRJ

The Good I Am seeking is my health

Emma Curtis Hopkins
(Scientific Christian Mental Practice)

RAIN

Rain splatters against the window pane
I run out the door
I feel it against my skin
I close my eyes
Let the rain bathe me
I picture spirit
Cleansing my soul
Baptizing me anew
My soul is cleansed
I am released from the past
Free at Last

It cannot hurt me! Its rays bathe me in loving brightness. I choose to love the sun, as it loves me.

NRJ

To Love God is to see God in all

Emma Curtis Hopkins
(Scientific Christian Mental Practice)

SUN

Blessing from the heavens
A Golden Flame on the Horizon
Nourishing the earth
Sun drenched skin
It is a showering of love from above
Others try to deceive
Wanting you to believe
Pain is its effect
Look to what is true
God can only love you

Your words have fed me. Given me Eternal Life.

NRJ

Love is the Good we are seeking

Emma Curtis Hopkins
(Scientific Christian Mental Practice)

NOURISH

The Soul fills our being
Craving, yearning
Wanting to be fed
The Knowledge of wisdom and
understanding
Vibrating through every core
Nourishment from the Lord
Gives the spring to your step
The Smile on your face
Makes the world a better place
Nourish your neighbor
With a kind word
And watch as the world
Starts working together

Two souls coming together to make One, unified by the Universe blessing the world.

NRJ

God works through Truth

Emma Curtis Hopkins
(Scientific Christian Mental Practice)

TWIN FLAME

Living worlds apart
Two Flames ignite
A chosen path to unite
Unseen forces try to keep them apart
Faith in what is true
Will see them through
God's plan is at hand
They are on a mission
With one ambition
To unite as one
Under the blazing sun

The Father and I are One. Can there be anything greater. Love is the greatest power. Choose to love instead of hate. Let us heal this world.

NRJ

I Am my own understanding of God

Emma Curtis Hopkins
(Scientific Christian Mental Practice)

LOVE

Seeking Love
You look around
It is no where to be found
Under a Tree?
Behind a Bush?
Within a Flower?
Nope, it isn't there either
You sit in the silence
A sound within
Beckons you to come in
A pink flame
Is what you see
A warm fuzzy feeling
That will set you free
It was there all along
Just waiting for you to hear its song

Spirit and I come together to form One. We can never be separated. Truth and love bind us together for all time.

NRJ

I Am power of life to the Universe

Emma Curtis Hopkins
(Radiant I AM)

ONE

Black, white, Red, yellow
What colors do you see?
I see the children of Tomorrow
Around the world
With one Breath
Conception takes place
Nestled in the womb of mothers
Souls begin to Sprout
Lives are taking form
All created by the One
One breath, One Life
What colors do you see?
I only see the One

Believe in yourself. Seek and ye shall find. Truth.

NRJ

The first Angel is the first to look up

Emma Curtis Hopkins
(High Mysticism)

ANGEL

Angels come in many forms
A Friend, a stranger…..
They will guide you through a storm
Making sure that you are kept safe
and warm
They will heed your call
When you feel you're about to fall
They'll be with you on every journey
Helping you to fulfill your destiny
A blessing in disguise
So keep your eyes on the prize
When you're looking for an Angel
Many of God's Creations
Are waiting for your command
To lend a helping hand

I see the face of angels everywhere.

NRJ

You know there is a natural strength

Emma Curtis Hopkins
(Scientific Christian Mental Practice)

POWER

I plant a seed
Watch it grow
Into a wonderful beautiful flower
As I grow
And learn to know
God is all I see
I Am ready to be me
All challenges and errors
Something trying to create terror
Has no place within me
Ceases to be
From what I was have learned
Everything I have earned
All Power is given unto me
I rejoice with glee
My Power is Gods Power

Everything you want to accomplish can be done now.
You are just getting started.

NRJ

Let your flowing thoughts warmed at the fountain of pure reason, be rich in affection, love, life, and harmony

Emma Curtis Hopkins
(Scientific Christian Mental Practice)

TIME

They say time is of the essence
Not in the eye of the Almighty Presence
I move with grace and ease
Knowing I hold the keys
My destiny at hand
Will be surveyed throughout the land
I have nothing to prove
I Am making all the right moves
Time is mine

I move with the rhythm of life that I create. Guided by love, I Am happy.

NRJ

I Am the Resurrection and the Life

Jesus Christ

DANCE

As I move to the beat
I feel a pulsating heat
Urging Me
To fill every note
I seem to fall into a trance
Spirit moving my body to dance
I feel free
Spirit speaking to me
Flowing with my every move
I feel love

www.ingramcontent.com/pod-product-compliance
Lightning Source LLC
Chambersburg PA
CBHW042126080426
42734CB00001B/9